Getting
Rid
of the
What Ifs?

Getting
Rid
of the
What Ifs?

MICHAEL TRAINA

FIVE KIDS
PUBLISHING

DOYLESTOWN, PENNSYLVANIA

5 Kids Publishing
105 Montgomery Avenue, Suite 1053
Lansdale PA 19446

978-0-9904793-0-7 Print book
978-0-9904793-1-4 E-book

PCIP available on request

CONTENTS

Introduction   1

1   It's All in Your Head!   6

What Is Happiness?   6

What If You Could Feel Like This Every Day?   7

Listen to Your Mind   9

In the Moment   10

Thoughts Are Negative or Pessimistic   11

Thoughts Are Not Facts: The "What If" Factor   12

True Happiness   13

What Can You Be?   15

2   Your Mind Told You What?   16

The First Twenty Seconds   16

Observe Your Thoughts   17

Don't Buy What Your Mind Is Selling   18

Stop the Train   19

Through the Mouse Hole   20

No Thoughts at All or Positive Thoughts   21

3 "I Think I Can." The Power of
   Mantras   23

   Creating Your Mantra   24

   Different Thoughts = Different Outcomes   25

   My Experience with Mantras   27

   When to Use Mantras   29

   Mantras for Stressful Situations   30

4 Shhhh ... Making Your Mind Quiet 31

   What Is a Quiet Mind?   33

   Exercises to Calm Your Mind   34

    The Magic Bubble   34

    The Cloud   35

    The Blue Light   35

    Slow Motion   36

   Do Whatever Works   36

   Focused Times for Mantras and No Thoughts 37

    While Exercising   38

    While Driving or Traveling   38

    At Bedtime   38

    Finding Stolen Moments   39

   Use Active Time Wisely   40

   Two Ways to Happiness   41

   How Does This Work in My Life?   42

5 Roadblocks, Bad Days, and Setbacks — 44

Technology — 45

Media and Advertising — 47

Capitalism — 48

Work — 49

Family — 50

6 Your Mind Won't Go Down Without a Fight — 53

Your Mind Is a Rebel — 53

The No-Fun Syndrome — 54

Who Wants to Be Like That? — 55

Your Friends Won't Understand — 56

Catching Yourself — 58

Be Persistent — 58

Hard Times — 59

Be Committed — 59

Recognize Challenging Situations — 60

Don't Do It Now — 61

7 The Storm of Everyday Life — 62

Illness of a Loved One — 62

The Kids Won't Stop Fighting! — 63

The Daily Rush — 63

Your Finances — 66

I Don't Even Want to Get Out of Bed! — 67

My Loved One Is Annoying! — 67

I Hate My Job — 68

8 Answers to Your Questions   70

I am an Anxious Health Nut   70

When Will I Feel Calmer and Happier?   71

Obsessive Compulsive About Germs   72

I am Stuck   73

I am So Angry   73

I Have the Worst Headache   74

I Don't Want to Be Weird   75

I am Depressed   76

I Can't Listen to My iPod?   77

I Worry All the Time   78

My Life Is Getting Worse   79

Does This New Way of ThinkingConflict with My
    Religion   80

INTRODUCTION

I had it pretty good ... a great wife and a successful career. Surrounded by family and friends, I had healthy, happy children, and a warm, welcoming home, with family trips and golf on the weekends!

So why was I so miserable?

Even with all of the things that most people believe to be success, I never felt successful. I always wanted more, and I was never satisfied with what I had.

A former athlete and a very competitive person—I guess I "won" a lot—I never reveled in it. Instead, I thought, "Okay, now what's the next thing I have to do?"

Outwardly, I was the happiest guy around, but those closest to me found me difficult. My wife and I had a joke that if you wanted to really know me, you should watch the Easter video. Our family videotaped all of our holidays, and in each one, I was unsmiling, disengaged and just sitting there, going through the motions.

This book is the result of a long, personal journey that took me from being the miserable guy in the Easter video to someone who is more than simply happy. Today I enjoy a state of peacefulness and calm that I never knew existed.

I am sharing my journey now to prove to you that you can be happy while living a hectic, normal life. I have five kids at home and a stressful, seventy-hour-a-week job. The rest of my life is spent coaching my kids' games, wondering how I am going to pay the bills, helping sick relatives, breaking up fights between my kids, and trying to make sure my teenage daughter doesn't grow up too fast. *I am just like you.*

Although I do not live in a monastery, meditate for hours every day, or go on spiritual retreats, I have learned some simple changes and tools that have brought me calm amidst the chaos of my life, and I would like to share them with you.

I have found that the angst and lack of calm that we experience is caused by what I call the "what if" factor. We spend too much time living in a world of conjecture and wonder.

"What if I get sick?"

"What if I fail this test?"

"What if my boss doesn't like me?"

"What if I am never a success?"

"What if I get fired and can't take care of my family?"

All of these "what ifs" quickly go from just questions to becoming our reality and our permanent state of uncertainty and fear. In this book, I will help you rid yourself of the "what ifs" and the daily anxiety in your mind.

The Teachers

One of the critical things that changed my life was a movement that has taken hold in the United States, which is the search for happiness through Eastern philosophies including Buddhism, meditation, and the management of one's thoughts.

Writers such as Eckhart Tolle, Deepak Chopra, Wayne Dyer, Pema Chodron, Thich Nhat Hahn, Louise Hay, and others are wildly popular, and their books are bantered about in offices, classrooms, parties, and book clubs. As evidence of its growing popularity, Oprah Winfrey chose to include Eastern philosophy concepts on her TV shows. She even created a webcast series featuring Eckhart Tolle's book, *A New Earth*.

Millions of people, including me, owe a great debt to these thought pioneers. Through study and practice of their teachings, my life has been permanently changed for the better. My personal journey has led me to a point where I can say, without hesitation, that I believe these teachers are geniuses. Using their lessons to improve my life, I am happier and healthier than I have ever been.

One reason I wrote this book was to build a bridge between these great thinkers and people like you and me. I want to make their teachings accessible and make them work for you like they work for me. My purpose is to give you practical, real-life ways to be happy.

Tolle, Chopra, Dyer, and the others are considered by many to be outliers. They are not looked upon as mainstream people with mainstream problems. Many have spent considerable time in nontraditional lifestyles that include living in monasteries or quitting their jobs to study these philosophies.

The average person cannot relate to meditating with the Dalai Lama and spending days practicing silence, fasting, and abstinence. Also, their books are often difficult to understand. Combine hard-to-read, complicated concepts presented by nontraditional teachers and you can understand why people struggle to stay with them.

Most of us who have tried to follow these paths to happiness or enlightenment fall into two categories. One group wants to be happy and believes that some of the concepts in these books make sense, and yet, one might think, "How can I possibly follow the teachings in this book? I have four kids, an important job, and soccer games and birthday parties on the weekends. I don't have enough money, time, or energy to do all of this stuff!"

Others find that trying to read, understand, and implement the ideas can be very difficult—let's face it, these books are not exactly light reading. I often found myself having to reread sentences and paragraphs numerous times before I could grasp the concepts.

To make this book more relatable and useful, I included not only my own story, but also the thoughts and experiences of a diverse group of individuals. I interviewed a number of people to hear their voices and to learn about real struggles. I hope that you find yourself in these pages and realize that we all struggle with the same problems.

A former basketball player, I am the dumb jock who is attempting to make this stuff work for people like me, people who don't have the time, energy, or finances to retreat to a monastery to find peace of mind. We've got to find our happiness while we still pay the bills, cut the lawn, and get the kids on the school bus.

Armed with a master's in business administration, I have built multiple businesses to over $200 million in revenue, and at one point my company employed over 70,000 people in more than 140 offices nationwide. In spite of financial and entrepreneurial success, I knew that something was missing. This book is the result of a journey that has brought the kind of calm and happiness to my life that could not be found in material success.

When you read this book and follow the easy exercises, I promise that the quality of your life and the lives around you will vastly improve.

Together we will determine what is causing your anxiety and lack of calm, and you will be provided tools to help you get rid of the "what ifs." Scattered throughout the book, the exercises teach you how to identify and watch your thoughts, and how to change those thought patterns to more helpful ones. You will learn how to calm your mind and to avoid the behaviors, situations, and pitfalls that are roadblocks to making improvements.

1

IT'S ALL IN YOUR HEAD!

"Happiness is like a butterfly which, when pursued, is always beyond our grasp, but, if you will sit down quietly, may alight upon you."
—NATHANIEL HAWTHORNE, AUTHOR

What Is Happiness?

About half of the people who read and edited this book had a problem with my frequent use of the word happiness. They asked, "Aren't you really talking about calm, peace, or joy? You're not really talking about happiness, are you?"

I decided to keep the keep the focus on that word, because for the concepts in this book to be effective, my readers will need to redefine what happiness means to them, as I was able to do for myself.

I define happiness as the ultimate state of calm, a place where you don't want a thing and you don't feel that you need anything to make your life complete. Not achieved through getting more things or achieving a certain status, happiness can be yours whether you have everything or nothing. It is a place where the stories in your head stop, or at least become minimized.

What I am trying to get across is that you are truly happy when you are completely at peace. You are happy when you don't have anxiety, fear, worry, doubt, or depression. You are happy when you stop asking, "What if this happens or what if that doesn't happen?"

Do you think about happiness as excitement? Are you happy when you win a game, make more money, or meet a new friend? For the purpose of this book, I define those things as simply excitement, and I point out that they can be more harmful than good. When temporary excitement ends or gets boring, that can create a sense of wanting and can lead you to believe you will not be happy unless you get that feeling back. These "good" events can have negative effects.

Nevertheless, if you are reading the book and you find yourself getting stuck on the word happiness, ignore it or change it. Happiness is the word that works for me, but you may choose peacefulness, calm, joy, or some other word. No matter what word you choose, all of the concepts herein are the same and will work for you.

What If You Could Feel Like This Every Day?

Imagine being this person.

When I wake up in the morning, my mind is calm. I don't hate getting up. I am looking forward to the day. I am a baker, a plumber, or a CEO. I am a painter, a musician, a teacher, or a mother. This is going to be a great day.

I have a ton of energy. I am neither overwhelmed by life's problems nor by what I have to do today. I am happy as my kids get ready for school, and although the kids are fighting, my pace of life is calm and manageable and I can react to the arguments without thinking that my life stinks.

The kids get off to school and I leave for work or to do my daily routine, and I am not anxious or in a hurry. I am not worried about what I have to accomplish today.

I get to the office and the sight of my boss doesn't bother me. I am moving at a comfortable pace in spite of my stack of work, and I don't have thoughts about not being able to get my work done. I am not nervous, watching the clock and/or wondering when the day will end. I am simply happy doing one task at a time with my full attention. I am not trying to finish in order to move on to the next thing on my list.

I feel great. I do not have chronic pain. I am not worried about having a scratchy throat or about germs. I don't try to avoid door handles and faucets in public bathrooms, and I don't worry that the person preparing my food did not wash his hands. I feel strong and healthy, with every thought in my head supporting good health.

I am unconcerned about what people think of me, and I don't waste energy judging others. I don't care if I am rich enough, pretty enough, smart enough, or cool enough. I don't look at others as fat, ugly, rude, obnoxious, poor, or dumb. I see all people the same.

I am not worried about life's obstacles. I have enough money, a happy home life, a good my job, and I enjoy family activities.

I am neither worried, anxious, nor depressed. My wife

(or husband) is great, my kids are great, and I feel great. Today is a great day. I feel calm, energetic, and ready to enjoy life's options.

I've gotten rid of all the "what ifs" in my life.

I am happy.

> *"If I had my life to live over, I would perhaps have more actual troubles but I'd have fewer imaginary ones."*
>
> —DON HEROLD, HUMORIST,
> WRITER, AND ILLUSTRATOR

Listen to Your Mind

Do you ever just listen to your mind, really sit there and listen to your thoughts? Your thoughts tend to run in an endless, meandering path that you can hear as that little voice in your head or your own inner dialogue. Our minds will jump from one topic to another in the span of thirty seconds. You may go from "I wonder what I am going to eat for lunch" to "I think I might have cancer" to "I wonder if my wife is cheating on me because she bought a new dress."

When your mind operates in this way, it erodes your ability to be happy. If you pay attention and observe your mind and thoughts, you will notice three things:

1. Your mind is constantly thinking about things that are not related to what is going on right now.
2. Your thoughts are typically negative or pessimistic; seldom "in the moment," they are rarely positive.
3. Your thoughts are almost never facts. They are more

likely questions or assumptions that cause some form of anxiety. I call it the "what if" factor—what if this happens or what if that happens?

Let's break each one down.

In the Moment

Amy is the mother of three young boys. She describes her thought process like this: "I replay things in my head. My head doesn't stop, ever, ever, ever. I'll replay conversations I had with people. I think about what has to be done and what I didn't do. When I feel bad about something or if there's something with the kids, I think of it in advance of it happening. It doesn't stop. My brain doesn't stop."

Amy spends so much time replaying past events and anticipating future ones that it is hard for her to be happy in any current moment. Where in her thought pattern is: "I am really enjoying this moment. I feel great. I am enjoying spending time with my sons."

On the other hand, Christian, who is an entrepreneur and father of three, is pre-occupied with thoughts that focus on his business. He said, "If you manage a business, the process leads to projections for the future. Who should we hire or fire and when? What are next quarter's projected earnings? Will the new potential client actually order? And all the 'what ifs' are related to those questions. Certain business realities create mind patterns outside the present moment. I cannot seem to isolate the necessary future thoughts from the unnecessary future thoughts."

Another example comes from David, a retired educator. He describes his thoughts this way: "My transient concerns are not nearly so often looking ahead as they are looking back. I regret having made mistakes more than I am anxious about something that might happen. Last week in a golf match, I had a couple of bad breaks that struck at my confidence, I began to press, and my game never rallied. In short, I was letting the very recent past muck up the very near future. I was anticipating bad shots, not good shots."

Anticipating the worst is fairly typical. In my own life, I used to have a constant dialogue in my head, reviewing and analyzing problems, and I was never satisfied with what I had or what I achieved, even when one of my businesses was ranked by Inc. magazine as one of the fastest-growing businesses in the country.

Our minds tell us that happiness is not now, but will come in the future when we are doing something different. We can change that.

Thoughts Are Negative or Pessimistic

+ "What if I don't get the promotion?"
+ "What if my son doesn't just have a cold and is seriously ill?"
+ "What if my kid is taking drugs?"
+ "What if my parents don't like my boyfriend?"

When your thought pattern is negative, you can become anxious and depressed, creating scenarios in your head and replacing happiness with worry, doubt, and fear. For example, a busy mother of five, Kerry said, "I get bouts where I'm irrationally concerned about disease, whether it's the kids or me."

Amy related, "If my husband is five minutes late, the first thought that goes through my head is that he's been in an accident."

An executive and mother of two, Jennifer said, "I used to worry an awful lot about totally screwing up at work. And so anytime I'm in new situations, I have this really heightened feeling that I am out of my element. What if I screw something up that will have a material impact on the company?"

Unfortunately, when we don't analyze our thoughts, we allow them to become part of our daily lives, to become part of who we are. Our negative thoughts become our personalities. You choose the things you worry about the most and you become that person.

What would happen if we changed our negative thoughts to positive? What would happen if we didn't have negative thoughts at all?

Let's say "I am healthy" rather than "I must have a disease."

Thoughts Are Not Facts: The "What If" Factor

> *"If you want to test your memory, try to recall what you were worrying about one year ago today."*
> —E. JOSEPH COSSMAN, DIRECT MARKETER,
> ENTREPRENEUR, AND AUTHOR

The mind is tricky. We have all had this thought: "My throat is scratchy. I know I am going to get sick."

"I know I am going to get sick" is not a fact, but it is

something that we are saying in our heads. We worry about getting sick for minutes, hours, or days. We analyze every cough, scratch in our throat, pain in our body, or change in temperature. How can we possibly enjoy what we are doing if we are worried and anxious about being sick?

Your mind is very smart at distracting you, even though "I know I am going to get sick" is not a fact. Your mind treats it as a fact. You use words that turn it into a fact because the word "know" implies that it is a fact, when there is nothing factual about the entire sentence. You have now told yourself that it is a fact, and now you are going to get sick or at least spend a ton of time worrying about it because you "know" it to be true.

Take a look at the following sentences with the information you just learned.

- ✦ "I am definitely going to get sick from being around that sick kid."
- ✦ "I will never make enough money to buy the car I want."
- ✦ "I know I am not going to make these free throws."

Look at all the words we use to turn these sentences into facts:

- ✦ I am definitely
- ✦ I will never
- ✦ I know

What would happen if you changed the way your mind phrased those questions? Better yet, what if you never asked them?

True Happiness

"Each morning when I open my eyes I say to myself: I, not events, have the power to make me happy or unhappy today. I can choose which it shall be. Yesterday is dead, tomorrow hasn't arrived yet. I have just one day, today, and I'm going to be happy in it."

—GROUCHO MARX,
AMERICAN COMEDIAN AND ACTOR

How can you be happy if you can't focus on what's going on right now? How can you be happy if your thoughts and words are negative, convincing you that something is true when it is not true?

We think that being happy has to do with all the stuff going on in our lives, when it really has to do with how we think or don't think about it in our minds. Reread that sentence—it is the key to happiness.

Happiness is not a result of what's going on. Happiness is how we think about what's going on.

You are not unhappy because you have no money or because you are not rich enough. You are happy or unhappy based on how you think about your financial situation. Change your thought pattern to enjoy true happiness.

I used to set goals for myself that were way out in the future, where I thought happiness would exist for me. Consumed with the future, I would think, "I'll be happy when I have $1 million in the bank and when my stock price goes through the roof. I'll be happier when I sign that deal. I'll be happier when my kids are older."

I have learned to change this thought pattern and to harness the power of my mind to bring true happiness to my life, and you can too. Here are the basic building blocks that helped me find happiness:

+ Become aware of your thoughts and calm your mind. Don't let your thoughts make you miserable.
+ Use mantras to train your thoughts.
+ Use breathing and visualization to experience calm and find happiness.
+ Eliminate the "what ifs."

What Can You Be?

+ You can be happy at all times regardless of your life circumstances.
+ You can be free of worry and anxiety.
+ You can stop judging people.
+ You can stop caring if people judge you.
+ You can be immune to other people's actions and comments.
+ You can stop being afraid.
+ You can stop trying to control every life experience for you and your loved ones, by just letting it happen.
+ You can stop doing things that provide temporary excitement but lead to long-term unhappiness and regret.
+ You can be happy.

1

YOUR MIND TOLD YOU WHAT?

"If you don't like something change it; if you can't change it, change the way you think about it."

—MARY ENGELBREIT,
CHILDREN'S BOOK AUTHOR

The First Twenty Seconds

The first step on the road to happiness is to set expectations for what you want. To achieve calm, peace, and happiness you must expect that you can, believe it, and have faith. To bolster that belief and faith, affirm and celebrate your victories and your progress.

Start by trying to be happy for only twenty seconds. When you can be happy for twenty seconds, you can be happy for an hour, and when you can be happy for an hour, you can be happy for a day. And, if you can be happy for a day, you can be happy all year.

The hardest part and the easiest part are the first twenty seconds. I am going to show you how to get twenty seconds of happiness no matter what is going on in your life. You might be broke, you might be sick, you might be depressed, but if you know how to get twenty seconds, you know how to do it for the rest of your life.

Remember, we are not going for the thrill of the big win; we are going for a state of calm, with no anxiety.

Observe Your Thoughts

For your first twenty seconds, start by watching your thoughts. Right now, set this book down and "listen" to the thoughts that are going through your mind. Actually tune in and listen to the voice in your head.

What is your mind saying to you? Maybe your thoughts went something like this: "This guy is crazy. What is he talking about? Watch your thoughts? I don't have any thoughts, and if I do that's just who I am. Why would I ever stop my thoughts? Who would I be? I would be like a zombie."

Or maybe your thoughts were more like Kerry's. She described her thought patterns like this: "I noticed while watching my thoughts that I tend to go back and replay conversations in my mind. It can be a passing conversation or a more in-depth talk, it doesn't seem to matter, it's more of a commentary. I guess I don't even shut up in my own mind!"

In past years, my own thought patterns were similar, with constant dialogue in my head, reviewing and analyzing problems. Your thoughts could simply run to the mundane, such as: "What will I make for dinner? I hate making dinner. I never know what to cook. The kids never appreciate all the effort I make."

The key is to constantly watch your thoughts. As I mentioned earlier, contrary to what one might think, most of our thoughts are negative and cause fear, anxiety, depression, distrust, doubt, or anger. When you pay attention to your thoughts and recognize negative patterns, they will begin to go away or at least slow down.

Another reason to observe your thoughts is to become conscious of the types of things that you think about and the types of things that you worry about.

Kerry concluded: "When I first started watching my thoughts, I found it very unnerving and really thought I must be nuts. I thought that, of course, everyone had thoughts, but that I had way more than anyone else. Now, I know that everyone has crazy thoughts, and, for some reason, I find that comforting."

Don't Buy What Your Mind Is Selling

"Every thought is a seed. If you plant tomatoes, don't expect to grow peaches."
—UNKNOWN

Now that you are watching your thoughts, you can begin to analyze what you are thinking and how many of your thoughts are facts; you may notice that this is a very small number. Make a commitment to yourself that you will allow only those thoughts that actually true. For example, you may think to yourself: "I wonder if I am sick. My throat is scratchy. I must be sick. I bet I got sick from standing out in the rain or maybe from babysitting the two-year-old."

Notice that not one of those thoughts is a fact, and if you just let them happen without changing them, you may believe that they are true and that you are, in fact, sick. When you stop and analyze and accept only true facts, the number of your harmful thoughts will decrease.

The busy mother of three, Amy said: "My thoughts are not always negative, although they are rarely positive. My thoughts this week consisted mostly of thinking about what has to be done that day, the next day, and the rest of the week. What if someone is getting sick? How will that affect the week? Will everyone get sick? Will there be an asthma episode? What medicine should everyone be taking? Am I getting sick?"

Does thinking about her children's potential (not factual) illnesses do anything to enhance Amy's level of happiness and calm? No, her mind has created a thought pattern that can lead to stress and anxiety—and none of that is based on a single fact.

Jennifer described these feelings at work: "As I watched my thoughts, I saw that they tend to speed up when I face conflict. Then I ask myself all sorts of questions that generally discount someone else's perspective. Is he crazy? How can she think that? She has no clue!"

Stop the Train

A huge step in the search for happiness is "stopping the train."

Have you ever heard the phrase, "stop the train before it leaves the station"? It's easy to stop a train when it isn't moving, but once it gets going with a full head of steam, it is not so easy to stop it—just like your train of thoughts.

For example, when Amy's sons were diagnosed with asthma that upped the stakes when they come down with a cold or a respiratory illness, leading Amy to a great deal of anxiety when one of the boys even sneezed. Here she describes a typical scenario: "My husband came upstairs and said, 'Sean has a runny nose' and I instantly got a knot in my stomach. I thought, 'What's his action plan? Do we need to start with his medication? What do we have planned? Is this going to interfere with his birthday party? Is it the flu? All of this is going through my head all at one time."

Amy's train had clearly left the station. If she had watched her thoughts and stopped the train at "what is his action plan?" she would have recognized that none of the questions were based on facts and therefore, they made her anxious and detracted from her happiness. If she had thought, "I'll have his action plan ready," the train would have stopped before it left the station.

True happiness is achieved by stopping the train before your thoughts run away from you. Here is an exercise to help you stop the train.

Through the Mouse Hole

This is a great technique to isolate your thoughts. Picture a mouse hole in your mind and imagine that every thought must come through the mouse hole. As each thought flows through, try to categorize it as negative, anxious, depressed, or a fact.

When you do this for a week, you will begin to categorize your most common thoughts and you will notice that the stream of constant thoughts will slow down. Now, commit to allowing only true facts to come through; tell yourself that if the thought is not a fact, you will not allow it through the hole. Notice that your mind will slow down and you will feel calmer.

No Thoughts at All or Positive Thoughts

Once you start to observe your thoughts, the next step is to work toward a state of no thoughts or positive thoughts. No matter the situation around you, you will maintain no negative or harmful thoughts.

Here is an extraordinary example to make the point: your wife calls you to let you know that your son has been kicked out of school, he got caught with drugs, and you must come home from work immediately—she needs you home now.

As you hop in the car, your mind starts racing: "I can't believe he did that. I am going kill him. He has always been my troublemaker. I am going to ground him for a year. He is never going to be able to get into another school. He just ruined his life. The entire neighborhood is going to know. We are going to be the laughingstock of the entire town. What are we going to do? We might have to move. I knew my wife was always too easy on him. I bet he was hanging out with that one friend who has always been bad news."

The thought pattern continues until you get home and you arrive filled with anxiety, worry, embarrassment, stress, and fear. And through all of these thoughts, what did you gain? Did these thoughts help you?

Instead, what if you simply repeated thoughts such as: "My son has always been a good kid. This situation will work itself out. I have faith in my wife and kids. I love my son."

With this state of mind, would your mood be changed? Would you feel calmer and happier? Do you feel better when you don't allow your negative thoughts to wear on you and bring you down?

Alternatively, what if you stopped all of the negative thoughts and tried to have no thoughts at all. Driving home in a complete sense of calm, every time a negative thought entered your mind, you stopped it and had no thoughts. By not allowing the anxiety about the event to control your mood or your thoughts, you let it all occur without disrupting your happiness. Under each of the three approaches, the facts of the situation never changed. Remember, it is not the situation that causes anxiety, but instead, our anxiety is determined by how we think about the situation.

I bet right now you're saying that I am crazy and it is impossible to do. Managing your thoughts is difficult and it takes work, but it is far from impossible. When you master this process, your life will change.

3

"I Think I Can." The Power of Mantras

"I think I can ... I think I can ... I think I can ..."
—*The Little Engine That Could*

Do you remember the children's book *The Little Engine That Could?* Pulling the long, heavy train over the mountain, that little engine had an impossible job, but, by repeating the now-famous phrase, "I think I can," the little engine put mind over matter and succeeded. This is the power of mantras.

Simple and potent tools, mantras are repeated words or phrases that help you program your mind toward positive thoughts and away from negative ones. Another word for mantra is affirmation.

You can repeat your mantra aloud or silently in your head. As we've discovered, the thoughts in our head are often negative. Repeating a positive mantra is an active approach to replacing those negative thoughts with positive ones. We can all benefit from the example of boxer Muhammad Ali, who said, "I figured that if I said it enough, I would convince the world that I really was the greatest." It worked.

Creating Your Mantra

*"Any thought that is passed on to the
subconscious often enough and convincingly
enough is finally accepted."*

ROBERT COLLIER, AUTHOR OF
SELF-HELP BOOKS, INCLUDING
THE SECRET OF THE AGES

For your mantra, choose a positive word or phrase that has meaning for you, something that you can say over and over. It can be a state of mind or a state of being to which you relate or aspire to achieve; for instance, a simple mantra might be: "I am happy."

Everyone has certain personality traits and/or mind patterns that become their most destructive characteristics. Some people are anxious, some are depressed, some worry about health, some hate their bodies, some are angry.

When you create your mantra, look at yourself and be very honest about what type of person you are and what type of negative thoughts you have. Your mantra will put a positive spin on your most common negative thoughts. Once you learn to watch your thoughts, you will find it easier to figure out what your mantra should be.

Obsessively worried about her children's health, Amy started using the mantra, My children are happy and healthy.

A businessman, father, and recreational coach who often finds himself frantically rushing from one activity to the next, Warren used his mantra to help refocus his attention.

He explains, "One popular mantra for me in a crisis or rush is 'what's great about this situation?' This helps me relax and pull the positives out of any circumstance."

I suggest that your mantra be something easy to remember, short to say and think, and easily repeatable, as you may be repeating it five hundred times a day. You can and should repeat your mantra as much as possible.

For my mantra, I find four thoughts too many to remember and two thoughts not enough to focus on. Here are some ideas that you can use alone or combine:

"Today is a great day."
"I love myself."
"I am healthy."
"I am prosperous."
"Today is a great day for my career."
"I love my job."
"I am successful."
"I am happy."
"I forgive myself."
"I forgive others."
"I live only in the present."
"I release all guilt."
"I do not judge others."
"I am at peace."

Imagine if all of your thoughts were some combination of those on this list, instead of the series of negative thoughts that your mind tends to produce. Determine the mantra that works for you and say it throughout the day and anytime you have a negative thought. How different would you feel if these positive ideas were your thoughts, every day?

Different Thoughts = Different Outcomes

> *"The repetition of affirmations lead to belief.*
> *And once that belief becomes a deep conviction,*
> *things begin to happen."*
>
> CLAUDE M. BRISTOL, AUTHOR OF
> PROSPERITY CLASSIC
> *THE MAGIC OF BELIEVING*

Mantras will help you think differently about yourself and your goals. You will notice that all of the mantras in the previous section are very affirmative, as if they are already true. State all of your mantras as if they are facts, even if they haven't yet happened.

Imagine how things might have turned out had the Little Engine said, "There's no way I can do that!" or if Muhammad Ali's oft-repeated phrase was "I might be pretty good" instead of "I'm the greatest!"

When your mind treats negative statements as facts, try to create positive statements that your mind can believe; this will result in the opposite of a negative self-image.

Remember, the person who says, "I will never be rich and I will never be thin" never will. To change that mindset, begin to train your mind using mantras that assume your goal has already happened. When your mind tells you that you are fat and that you hate your job, you can counter those thoughts with a positive mantra such as:

"I love my body."
"My job is perfect."
"I am healthy and strong."

This power of positive thinking is the basis of the popular book, *The Secret*. The author, Rhonda Byrne, suggests that if you plant seeds in your subconscious, your mind will make them come true. The book uses this concept to help people try to get everything that they want, based on the idea that what you imbed in your subconscious will come true; that is, if you think you are sick, you will get sick, if you think you are successful, you will be.

As a result, I suggest that one of your mantras should refer to something that you want to be true in the future, either a specific or a broad goal or a desire. Some ideas for future-related mantras are:

"I will be safe and secure when I retire."
"My kids will be successful."
"I will be prosperous."

My Experience with Mantras

My own experience with mantras has consisted of two parts. The first is situational and the second is trying to determine a constant, intensively positive thought pattern. As it relates to the first type of mantra, if I am in a stressful situation, I try to create mantras around that. When I am starting to feel stressed or ego-driven about my job or something at work, I try to let go of those thoughts by using mantras like these:

"I release all attachment to my stock price."

"I let go of any ego associated to my role as CEO."

I have also used mantras related to my self-perception. When you practice and believe in mantras and positive thoughts wholeheartedly, you will realize that a lot of your conditioning may have caused low self-esteem and harmful thoughts about yourself and your real value. I use mantras such as:

"I love myself."

"I love my life."

"I love my health, my family, my being."

These are not very macho phrases, and not the kinds of mantras that a jock and fraternity guy like myself would typically say to himself! And yet, I have found them to be very, very helpful.

All of the barriers that your mind puts up, all of those facades—"I am cool," "I am athletic," "I am better than that guy," "I am smarter than that guy"—stem from the fact that you want to feel that you are better than others because you don't feel secure about yourself. These are not true feelings, but simply conditioned feelings.

Some of my mantras are around trying to "uncondition" all of those feelings that have been built up over the years. No matter what happens, whether I get the contract or I don't get the contract, whether my kid makes the NBA or gets cut from the eighth-grade team, using my mantras I feel good about myself, about my family, and about life.

You can say outwardly, "I am the greatest guy in the

world." And yet, your subconscious will whisper your real feelings, thoughts, and beliefs. Maybe you really believe that you are the greatest guy in the world, while you think that you have a lot of faults. Your mantras are powerful tools with which to turn those negative thoughts into positive thoughts. Each stated as a fact, these mantras are positive thoughts about life, aspirations, and goals:

> "I am healthy, I am prosperous, I achieve my goals."
> "I forgive myself."
> "My family is healthy and everyone supports each other."
> "I love myself, I release all guilt, I am happy."

What happens when you put mantras to work for yourself? Are your thought patterns beginning to improve?

Amy describes her experience repeating the mantra, "My children are happy and healthy." She said, "It helped calm me and slow my thought pattern. When I felt myself tense up, I said the mantra and it actually made me focus my attention elsewhere, which for me is always good. This was a positive mantra for me, as it helped push away the negative thoughts."

When to Use Mantras

Use your mantras as often as possible!

Now that you know how to watch your thoughts and use mantras, you will start to realize that a significant number of your thoughts are negative or irrelevant. Nevertheless, you will still have times when your thoughts get away from you and you catch yourself having negative thoughts that distract you from what you are doing. When this happens, repeat your mantra over and over again in your head until the harmful thoughts slowly disappear. Over time and with practice, your mantra will become the dominant thought in your mind and negative thoughts will vanish.

Eventually, you will say your mantra constantly without having to think about it—your thoughts will become your mantra and you'll disregard bad thoughts altogether, while your mantra fills your mind. When you watch and evaluate your thoughts and use mantras, you will have a more positive outlook and a happier daily life.

This change of thought pattern from negative to mantra should be done all day, at work, in the shower, in church, at parties, during baseball practice, and before you go to sleep. If you struggle with getting other thoughts to disappear, try saying the mantra out loud. Try to find a private place for this, such as in your car when you are driving by yourself. Of course, if someone pulls up next to you, they will think you are crazy, but saying your mantra out loud really works to focus your mind.

Mantras for Stressful Situations

I suggest that you create a daily mantra that works on your most prevalent negative thoughts. However, you will often have situations arise that create temporary thought patterns that take over and are stronger in the moment than your normal thoughts.

For instance, suppose you get into a car accident. While

the police are arriving and you are calling your spouse, a whole series of negative thoughts will occur that have nothing to do with your typical pattern. I call these situational thoughts, and they require situational mantras. At those times when you see a new, negative thought pattern creep in, use a mantra that fits the situation. Suppose your normal mantra is, "I am healthy, I am prosperous, and I am calm."

At the crash site, you may have a deluge of new, negative, situational thoughts: "My insurance premiums will go up. I will never be able to afford insurance. My husband is going to kill me, he already thinks I don't know how to drive. What if I get too many points and lose my license? This guy's insurance card looks fake. Is he going to flee the scene and leave me holding the bag?"

When your mind heads down this path, pause and focus on your thoughts, which may be racing away with you like a runaway train. At such stressful times, create a mantra to address the situation, such as: "I am safe and secure. Accidents are an acceptable part of life."

This type of mantra will not change the situation—you will still have had an accident—yet, armed with a mantra, your mind will not be making the accident situation even more shocking than it is, causing you to go into hysterics and making a bad situation worse. Remember, situational mantras are temporary, and once the situation is back to normal, you can return to your usual, everyday mantra; just be ready to change it when the need arises.

In high-pressure situations, you can always fall back on this mantra to help reduce negative, anxious thoughts:

"I release all negative thoughts."

4

Shhhh ... Making Your Mind Quiet

"Only in quiet waters things mirror themselves undistorted. Only in a quiet mind is adequate perception of the world."

HANS MARGOLIUS,
GERMAN PHILOSOPHER AND AUTHOR

Once you have mastered mantras and feel that you have reasonable control of your thoughts and their content, the next step is to try to eliminate your thoughts altogether. What does that mean? I am referring to a calm mind that allows for clear thinking about the facts at hand; I am not talking about a permanent state of unconsciousness!

I want you to eliminate transient thoughts that are based in faulty assumptions or premises. With practice, you can also eliminate the need to have positive thoughts or mantras.

You are trying to get to a state where you are completely present and engrossed in your surroundings and what is going on in the moment. When your mind is consumed with the present, you don't have time to worry, fear, panic, or hypothesize.

The goal is to stop analyzing each and every event: "Why did she do that?" Instead of judging events as they occur, you will learn to let things happen and relate to them without thoughts.

What Is a Quiet Mind?

A truly quiet mind creates the ultimate level of happiness and calm that, believe it or not, is a state of no thoughts. When you have no thoughts, you are not replacing bad thoughts with good thoughts; instead, you replace them with nothing. Nothingness is the ultimate achievement.

For example, if you have negative thoughts about your boss, notice them, stop them immediately, and replace them with nothing—creating a state of calm and quiet. Just continue to do whatever you were doing without anxiety created by your mind and your thoughts.

If you were thinking about your boss while getting a cup of coffee, stop thinking about your boss and just get your cup of coffee. This may be very difficult to do and takes practice, yet it is well worth investing the time it takes to figure out how to do it.

The traditional way to get to a place of no thoughts is to concentrate on breathing in and out. Focus on every breath you take and how it feels and sounds. This may sound silly, yet if you really focus, all of your thoughts will disappear and you will be calm and happy, in the moment, at the coffee machine, with no thoughts about your boss. Just coffee and that's it. True happiness.

I make my mind go blank. When I have a thought—
"Oh, I cannot believe that guy did that at work today!"—I
try to stop myself at "I cannot believe ..." and go to blank.
I watch for the next thought and I try to extend the period
of time between the last word I thought and the next word
that came to mind. I elongate that period by focusing on my
breath, in and out, and extending the out breath for as long
as possible, with no thoughts.

Exercises to Calm Your Mind

During the pace of a busy day it may be hard enough
to maintain calm and positive thoughts, let alone trying to
stop them completely. Visualization exercises may help you
to quiet your mind and eventually get to no thoughts. Here
are four exercises that you can do on the run or even while
the kids are running around the house, shouting at each
other, or making a mess.

The Magic Bubble

To quiet your mind, pretend that you are inside a bubble,
warm, safe, and comfortable. You are almost weightless. The
bubble can be any color, as long as it is transparent.

Now, visualize that no thoughts can enter the calm,
quiet bubble; all of your thoughts are outside the bubble.
Imagine thoughts trying to get in, and failing. You will find
that this works great when there is tremendous chaos going
on around you—you can visualize or maybe even see the
chaos outside the bubble.

Try changing the bubble to be the area where you are physically located at the moment. For instance, make your car the bubble while you are driving; watch your thoughts and don't let them enter the car. For a calming exercise, try making a room, your office, or your back porch into your bubble, where thoughts are not allowed to enter.

The Cloud

One way to separate yourself from your thoughts is to literally separate yourself from your mind and rise above your thoughts. Picture yourself sitting or laying on a cloud, and now picture yourself floating up on that cloud, high above all of your thoughts.

Imagine floating above your physical surroundings, far above your home and all the anxiety, worries, and thoughts associated with the people and things inside your house. Nothing below can bother you. Float above your town, your workplace, and the entire landscape below.

Above your anxiety, depression, fear, and wanting, you just observe the harmless thoughts stuck below you and your cloud.

The Blue Light

Similar to the bubble, the blue light has the ability to dissolve thoughts.

In this exercise, pretend that you are surrounded by blue light that is protecting you from thoughts. Any thought that is trying to get in through the blue light is dissolved and vanishes.

You can visualize the blue light anywhere and at any time—in the grocery store, at a kid's game, while you're jogging, or at work. When your mind is particularly active and hard to control, use the blue light to fight back and dissolve your thoughts.

Slow Motion

In this exercise, focus on each and every activity you are doing and give it your full attention, all in slow motion. When you pour a cup of coffee, focus on every detail. Pick up the pot slowly. Watch the coffee pour into the cup. How does the cup feel? Focus 100 percent of your attention on what you are doing at that exact moment. When you practice concentrating like this, your mind will calm tremendously.

Do Whatever Works

The four exercises above are just a few of literally thousands of ways to create visualizations that will help you control your thoughts. To find those that work best for you, try to keep it simple, without too many conflicting alternatives. Feel free to create your own visualization techniques, remembering that when choosing an exercise or creating one, try something that gives you a feeling of protection and separation from your thoughts.

Previously in this book, we read about David, a retired educator. David is also in the midst of a long battle with cancer. He said, "When I am feeling out of balance, grumpy, or overburdened by my thoughts, I am more abrupt and impatient, and I have physical reactions to my worries. When I was working, for example, I would periodically be unable to sleep. When I have behavioral manifestations or I'm unhappy, my wife sees it in my behavior."

At these times, David has learned to calm his mind with many techniques. He said, "One thing I often do is deep breathing. I try to empty my mind and relax on a bed in the dead man's position. I try to say, 'Hey, thanks, it's no effort just to lie here and calm down.' I also pray regularly."

Focused Times for Mantras and No Thoughts

"Empty your mind, be formless, shapeless— like water. Now you put water into a cup, it becomes the cup, you put water into a bottle, it becomes the bottle, you put it in a teapot, it becomes the teapot. Now water can flow or it can crash. Be water, my friend."
BRUCE LEE, MARTIAL ARTIST AND ACTOR

Repeating your mantras and creating periods without thoughts sound like great ideas and yet, we can get caught up in the pace of our lives and neglect to do our exercises. I like to find a number of times during the day when I can focus on my mantra and getting rid of all of my thoughts.

After periods of focused attention, repeating your mantra and slowing down your thoughts, perhaps while cooking dinner, changing the baby, or paying the bills, you will feel better and more calm and happy. I recommend practicing your mantra and calming techniques at certain times during the day when they are most effective, when your mind is free from other thoughts and the stress of the day is temporarily left behind. The following are examples of good times to create focused "mind time."

While Exercising

Physical exertion and exhaustion makes it hard for your mind to wander, so a great time to focus on your mantra and clearing your mind is during exercise, especially at the end of a hard workout. Repeating your mantra while you exercise ("I am happy, I am healthy") makes you feel good because your moments of calmness and "no thoughts" have no competition.

This is what they call a runner's high or being in the zone. Have you noticed that when all of your shots are falling on the basketball court or your putts are dropping on the golf course that you are calm, with no other thoughts? The exercise and physical fatigue enable you to focus.

While Driving or Traveling

While driving is a great time to focus, practice your mantras and visualization exercises, and clear your mind, with no distractions until you reach your destination—you will get there when you get there, and worrying will not get you there faster.

When I travel for work, dealing with traffic, airport security, car rentals, and more, I find that one of the best ways to reduce my stress and increase happiness is to forget about being late. I assume that something is going to happen to mess up my schedule, and when there are no delays, that's just a bonus. I don't worry about being late, and this approach has single handedly increased my happiness and reduced the number of negative thoughts I have while traveling.

At Bedtime

Bedtime is a perfect time to focus on your mantra and practice eliminating your thoughts. When you can't sleep because your mind is racing, watch your mind and reduce those extra thoughts. Whatever happened at work or at home, and what might happen, is irrelevant at this moment.

Regardless of whether your child is not getting good grades or hanging out with the wrong crowd, in bed you have unlimited time to focus on your mind—no reason not to do it at bedtime. If you are tired enough right before you fall asleep, your thoughts will slow down, in a way similar to exercise.

Use a mantra that keeps out all other thoughts, such as, "I have no negative thoughts," and you will find that you fall asleep faster and sleep better.

Finding Stolen Moments

Stolen moments are my favorite time for focusing on the mind and my thoughts. During these moments I am able to consciously focus on my mind and, therefore, I am more attentive to what I am doing. What is a stolen moment? It is anytime where one can sit quietly without distraction and spend focused time on what's going on in the mind.

One of my stolen moments is at my desk, where, instead of sending e-mail, I take five minutes and focus on my mind and my mantras; then, I send the e-mail.

Some of my other favorite times for stolen moments are in the bleachers at my kid's game, on airplanes, and sitting in my car before I enter the house. My wife loves to find her time while folding laundry.

When we are caught up in the "doing" of "doing," we don't take advantage of the many opportunities we have to make ourselves really happy and calm.

Of all of the "focus times" I have mentioned, stolen

moments are the most effective of them all for me. When I first started trying to change how my mind worked, I averaged about five stolen moments a week. I would go for days and then remember that I hadn't focused in a long time. As I got better at it (and subsequently more happy and calm), I began to average ten to twelve stolen moments per day. My goal is still to spend less time on distracted, wasted thoughts and more time with stolen moments, focused mantras, and a clear mind during exercise, at bedtime, and while driving and traveling.

Use Active Time Wisely

Often we stay distracted and unhappy because of our self-created, constant need to be doing things. Why? Because constant activity distracts us from the present moment. We mow the lawn, we wash dishes, we scrapbook, we download songs, we wax our car—we can't stop doing things, and during all of these activities, our mind is going nuts.

Analyze the activities you choose to engage in, making sure that they really need to be done, and that you are not using them as distractions that let your mind race. When you find yourself in a distracting, unnecessary activity, replace it with nothing.

Of course, the dishes aren't going to wash themselves and the grass will not be magically cut, but the next time you sit on your lawnmower, watch your thoughts. More useless thoughts will go through your head during that hour than you can possibly imagine: "I really need to trim those hedges. Why do my kids leave their toys all over the lawn?

Did we make the payment on the tractor? Who is that guy over there looking at me? Maybe I should put my shirt back on. I look fat."

Instead, use the hour of mowing the lawn as a stolen moment and focus on your mantra. Use the car wash as a place to do the bubble exercise. While you cannot take every moment of the day to be still and focus your mind, you can incorporate your mantras and exercises into many of your activities.

Two Ways to Happiness

There are two distinct paths to happiness: nothingness and positive thoughts. Which one works best for you? The ideal situation is to have no thoughts and simply live in calm and tranquility, with only thoughts that are factual: the trees are green, the sky is blue, the wind is warm.

However, calming your mind all the way to nothingness is difficult for most of us. Even the greatest yoga teachers who meditate every day find it a challenge to quiet their minds completely for long periods of time.

Based on my own experience, I believe that happiness is achieved through a progression over time. First, you change negative thoughts into positive ones by limiting the number of thoughts your have and replacing them with positive mantras. Once you succeed at this, you will enjoy a dramatic improvement in your quality of life.

Then, you can try to reach the state of no thoughts by practicing mantras every day and trying to achieve small gaps of time when you focus on nothing but your breath and clearing your mind. Focus on the breath alone, ignoring all of your thoughts, feel it go in and out, slow it down, listen to the in-and-out of your breath, and feel your stomach and lungs expand and contract.

At first, you might be able to manage only ten seconds of complete breath focus at a time, then gradually the amount of time and frequency of your focus will increase until, at any given time, you will have the ability to choose which path (mantras or no thoughts) to happiness you wish to take.

How Does This Work in My Life?

"The cyclone derives its powers from a calm center. So does a person."

NORMAN VINCENT PEALE,
MINISTER AND AUTHOR OF
THE POWER OF POSITIVE THINKING

When you incorporate all of these steps into your life, each and every experience will improve for you. When you can recognize your thought patterns, recite positive mantras, and clear your mind, you will find that tasks that you previously found stressful or unpleasant have turned into positive experiences.

Here is an example: You are giving a speech at work. You feel nervous, clammy, and ill. You stop and take a quick inventory of your thoughts and realize that you are thinking, "My palms are sweating, I don't feel well, I think I am going to faint; can my boss can tell I'm nervous?"

Right at that moment, you start reciting your mantra: "I am healthy, I am confident, I am successful" over and over in your head, and you feel better.

As you look around the room, you stop all of your negative thoughts as your mind clears and calms. You notice things about the room that in the past you had never seen because you were too nervous. You notice pictures on the wall, the lighting, and the layout of the tables. You look over your audience, and you see that your boss (the one you were worried about) isn't even in the room.

You have achieved a sense of calm and happiness in the moment. How do you think your speech will go when you are in that calm, confident, alert frame of mind?

> *"Peace is not something you wish for; it's something you make, something you do, something you are, something you give away."*
> —ROBERT FULGHUM,
> AMERICAN AUTHOR

5

ROADBLOCKS,
BAD DAYS,
AND SETBACKS

So you have decided that you want to be happier, calmer, and free from anxiety. You have tried all of the traditional methods to be happy—getting a better job, getting married, getting divorced, finding a new partner, making more money, downsizing, having kids, sending the kids to college—and none of it has worked.

You have read this book and decided that you have nothing to lose and are committed to trying. Like most people, your challenge may be that you want immediate results—just like most of us who are used to immediate gratification. So, what can you expect from following the approach in this book? Should you expect immediate happiness or a long, drawn-out process?

First and foremost, you should expect it to work. When you follow the processes outlined in the book, you will ultimately, although not immediately, achieve happiness. Determining your success will be the depth of your commitment, your beliefs, and how set you are in your old habits.

First, commit to your happiness by saying to yourself, "I believe in this process. It makes sense to me, and I am going to do it no matter what."

Second, believe in yourself and in the journey that you are about to take, even when your mind tells you that this is nonsense and you don't need it. Your mind will challenge you. To achieve your goals, you must continue to believe in them and not give in to old thought patterns.

Lastly, you will let go of your old habits when you change the way you think and behave. However, if you only jump into the process half way, then you will get "half-way results." Getting in the way of your intentions and impeding your progress may be such influences as cravings, pervasive technology, alcohol, drugs, having to be the life of the party, judging people, and a tendency to worry. Even if you continue those behaviors, you will have results, but not great results. Replacing old habits with new ones is the key to your new happiness.

Roadblocks will undoubtedly pop up. Here are some of the most common ones to watch for and try to avoid.

Technology

You may not want to hear this, but I believe that TV, computers, iPads, smartphones, social media, and all those other electronic devices are only preventing you from being happy—they are all the ultimate distractions. The key to happiness is to eliminate distractions that take your mind away from the present moment and fill it with negative or useless thoughts.

A perfect example of such a distraction is text messaging. When you are driving and engaged in a texting conversation with someone (of course you shouldn't be texting and driving anyway), where are your thoughts? "What am I going to say next? Let me try to type this while I am driving. Why hasn't she answered? I hope she isn't offended. I shouldn't have said that. Shall I text back or wait?"

Very likely, little about the text conversation was related to creating happiness, clearing your mind of negative and useless thoughts, or promoting a positive mantra.

How about TV? As a society, we watch hours and hours of television every day. Although I am not against TV because it dulls our brains cells and makes us lazy, I am against it because it occupies our minds, makes our minds race, and distracts us with useless information. TV can also increase your level of anxiety and fear when you watch the daily news, videos of disasters and violence, horror movies, and sad stories.

Of course, avoiding technology completely is impossible, so I recommend that you limit time spent on your various electronic devices, and when you do use them, focus 100 percent of your attention on what you are doing rather than letting them distract you from the moment. For instance, don't leave the TV on while eating dinner or working around the house. Don't turn the radio on in the car just to have it on, don't text while you're doing something else, and don't walk around with your iPod on while you are doing other activities. When you're in the mood for music, focus 100 percent of your attention on listening. When watching TV, focus on what you are watching instead of using TV as background noise.

Limiting your use of technology may be challenging, and yet, when you try it, you will find that useless thoughts decrease and your anxiety levels drop. I guarantee that after a few months, you won't even miss it!

Try this. Instead of turning on the TV tonight, take a half hour to focus on your thoughts and mantras. Do that for two weeks and see how great you feel.

Media and Advertising

The exposure to and impact of media and advertising go hand in hand with technology—very little of it contributes to our happiness. Very few TV shows, magazine articles, advertisements, or even "feel-good" stories benefit our happiness and ourselves. Certainly there are valuable programs and sources of information. It is critical to choose wisely and thoughtfully which programs and media outlets to which you will devote your attention.

Realizing the previous paragraph may be difficult to digest, let me provide more insight. Most media exist to influence your thoughts, feelings, and opinions, which are not facts. Media simply disseminate more information for you to cling to and with which to create negative thought patterns. Remember the three things our minds, and most media, do to create unhappiness: They focus on the past or the future instead of the current moment, they dwell on negativity, and they fill your head with everything but facts.

How much time did the whole world spend on fears about Y2K, the concept that in the year 2000 all computers would shut down because they were not equipped to roll their calendars over from 1999 to 2000? Billions of dollars and years of worry were spent on this issue. Media hype promoted the idea that Y2K might mean the demise of the entire U.S. economy. Then, 2000 came and nothing happened, except that I drank too much champagne.

Now, advertising. Pharmaceutical company ads are a great example of my point. Have you heard this commercial?: "Do you feel sluggish? Are you tired? Do you have chronic pain? Do you feel anxious? Depressed? If you have any of these symptoms, then you may need our drug."

Ads like this one are harmful to our happiness because they validate our fears and anxieties by creating worry about all of these symptoms. How might we feel if we didn't hear that commercial? We certainly would feel no worse than we felt the moment before we heard it.

How about the feel-good story about the child with the rare form of cancer that got better and is doing great now? Distracted from the current moment, we spend time lamenting over the story and worrying about how it relates to our children's health. How many times have you seen something on TV and then wondered if you or your children or spouse may have similar ailments or medical problems?

Capitalism

In our society, we learn that only the strong survive and that battles are won by the fittest. The people who have the most are the best, and those who have the least are the worst. Capitalism would have you believe that everyone is on a happy scale where the richest are at the top and the poorest are at the bottom, and many of our thoughts focus our attention on where we are on that scale. Nothing could be further from the truth.

You can enjoy what you are doing right now without a dime in your pocket. I can enjoy myself even if I am standing next to Bill Gates, even if I know that Bill is thinking to himself that I am a loser. I can be happy wearing a pair of jeans while standing next to a guy in a $1,000 suit.

I can enjoy myself in a 1984 pickup truck when I am at a stoplight next to a guy in a Ferrari. Getting in the way of my enjoyment are only my thoughts that I am not good enough, that my vehicle is a piece of junk, or that Bill Gates is talking about me to his friends—negative thoughts like these can consume us, when, in fact, none of those thoughts are facts.

Remember, you are not happy or unhappy based on what you have. Your happiness is determined by how you think about what you have and don't have.

Work

Most of us have to work for a living, and we can expect to spend forty hours a week, 2,000 hours a year for forty years—that's 80,000 hours over a lifetime. And, if you are a stay-at-home mom or dad, you will put in many more hours. While in the workplace, our minds are taking us away from the focus on, and satisfaction of, being in the moment. Our challenge is to find a way to enjoy our work.

Our minds tell us that work is what we have to do and it is difficult, unrewarding, and no fun. Once again, that is a spin that many of us have accepted as a fact.

We need to stop fighting every activity that we do. Right now, our minds fight activities. While we are at work, at a parent-teacher conference, or at our in-laws, our minds are taking us away from that moment. We need to be truly present at those events when they are taking place, or what is the sense of going? The truth is that the thing you are doing is not the thing that makes you happy or unhappy. It is the approach (how you think about the activity) that makes you happy or unhappy.

> *"One of my biggest problems is that I worked*
> *in a senior role for thirty-one years, a lot*
> *of time dealing with employees, coworkers,*
> *stakeholders, and so forth. I got very impatient*
> *with myopic or ideologically bound or patently*
> *selfish people, and some people were just*
> *impossible, and they'd go on my dartboard.*
> *All of this distracted me and took me out of*
> *balance. I wasn't thinking clearly and wasn't*
> *nearly as effective as I could have been."*
> —THOMAS, 61 YEAR OLD,
> FORMER LARGE COMPANY SENIOR EXECUTIVE

Family

Families are among the biggest contributors to a person's unhappiness, and not because a family causes unhappiness; in fact, it's quite the opposite. When our minds are constantly trying to worry about and ensure the happiness, safety, health, and prosperity of our families, we can't possibly achieve all that we want and hope for them and for ourselves.

To create calm and happiness in our minds regarding our families, we cannot be distracted by scenarios of danger, poor health, financial ruin, lack of success, disagreement, and disappointment. One way to pattern our thoughts to combat worry and anxiety surrounding family life is through the use of mantras, as described in Chapter 3.

By creating a series of positive family mantras we can calm the angst we feel regarding our family. Some mantras might include: "My children are safe and secure," "My family is healthy," and "My family is filled with love."

Another family-related topic is based on a perception of control or lack of control. We tend to allow our minds to let us believe that we have some degree of control over certain outcomes. We believe we can guide our children to successful sports careers, academic achievement, and good health. Although we can guide the activities, we cannot control the outcomes. Key to relieving the family-based anxiety is to detach from the outcomes we so desperately want because the reality is that the outcome will be what it is going to be.

For instance, we may start training our child to be a basketball player from the age of five. We teach them the proper shooting form, work on dribbling in the basement, enroll them in all the proper leagues, and even provide them with a personal coach. Many factors exist that will influence where our child ends up in the basketball world. Injury, interest, heredity, coaching, timing, growth, teammates, and more all play a role in what happens to them. In spite of our inability to control any of those factors, we spend an inordinate amount of time worrying about them. Having goals for your family and your children is prudent, but only once we detach from the outcomes can we truly be happy and, in turn, actually enjoy our family in a calm, "it will be what it will be" environment.

6

YOUR MIND WON'T GO DOWN WITHOUT A FIGHT

Your Mind Is a Rebel

Your mind does not want you to succeed. Remember, when you watched your mind, you found that many of your thoughts were negative. A constant theme throughout this book is the elimination of negative or transient thoughts; however, your mind won't go down without a fight.

Even if you are successful at quieting your thoughts, expect that, from time to time, your mind will try to bring you back to your negative patterns. In addition to all of your usual negative thoughts about your weight, your life, and your health, expect a new, most powerful negative thought pattern: the rebellion of your mind. Your mind will fight this process and try to convince you that it doesn't work.

Here are some of the thoughts to look out for: "This is stupid. How could I make myself happy just by changing my thoughts? This doesn't work. I don't feel any better. I give up. I was much happier before. I am going to go back to my old ways."

Be ready for the rebellion of your mind. When you realize that your mind is rebelling against the process, simply use the methods you have learned to focus on your mantra and to create a period of no thoughts. Keep in mind that these thoughts about the process not working are the same as other negative thoughts. They just appear to be more valid because you are learning to think differently.

The No-Fun Syndrome

Another version of rebellion of the mind is the "this is no fun" syndrome. The point of this book is to provide tools with which to break old thought cycles and create permanent happiness, and as it turns out, happiness is more about being calm and stress-free than it is about fun and excitement.

When I first started my own journey to happiness, I loved to have TV on in the background while I worked on the computer, and I texted all the time. It was my badge of honor to multitask and try to do numerous projects at the same time. I also drank when I was happy and I drank when I was stressed, because I thought that would increase my happiness and reduce my stress. I went to parties, competed with people at work, and dreamed about buying cool cars and having the nicest house on the block. All of this was supposed to be "fun."

All of these types of activities bring with them some level of stress, anxiety, jealousy, wanting, and a sense of lacking. Fun quickly turns into a negative feeling. We all associate fun with happiness, and fun can lead to excitement, but not lasting happiness. The "fun cycle" goes from fun to excitement to boredom to wanting, over and over again, in a constant struggle to combat what your mind is telling you.

When you give up the stress-producing things that you thought were supposed to be fun, your mind may tell you that you are no fun and that your new life is no fun. It's no longer fun to check out the BMWs at the car dealer and want one so you can show all your friends. It's no longer fun to want the nicest dress or the nicest lawn on the block. Your mind may tell you that you have become boring.

In fact, when you remove all of these "fun" distractions from your life, you calm your mind so you can be happy. Those distractions and "fun" were actually keeping you from being happy.

Your old habits will try to come back and your mind will try to convince you that, without all of those things, you aren't living—don't let your thoughts fool you.

Who Wants to Be Like That?

I have found that some people may be afraid that if this process works for them, they will lose their identity and all of the things about themselves that they love. Acknowledging that they may feel better, they are afraid that they will not be the same person they were before it all started.

You may wonder if you can still be funny, watch sports, be competitive, drive a nice car, tell dirty jokes, and hang out with the guys or your girlfriends. Some of the people who were interviewed for this book didn't want to go through the process if it meant they had to give up either the things they liked to do or the things they liked about themselves.

The great thing about the process of calming your mind and reducing the thoughts in your head is that it is a personal journey and you can do it in your own way, at your own pace, and to the extent that you want. This book makes a lot of suggestions, and they are just suggestions. While I recommend that you limit distractions, such as background noises from the TV or iPod, of course you can listen to your iPod and still have success. There is no one right way to calm your mind, and every exercise will not work the same for every person; for instance, some people prefer mantras to quieting the mind. All of the people involved in this book said, at one time or another, "I like that exercise better than this exercise" or "I just couldn't get that exercise." When you feel that way about an exercise, it is not a failure, it just doesn't work for you.

Your Friends Won't Understand

One of the most challenging roadblocks to trying a new path to happiness is the feeling that you are alone. Although the end result is worth it, it's possible that no one will understand what you are doing and why you are doing it. Many of your friends have the same negative mind patterns that you have, the patterns that you are trying to break. Once you try to break old habits by changing how you think and act, they may not understand, and they may begin to attack you with their own negative thoughts.

Our negative mind patterns affect how we interact with our friends, our family members, and our coworkers. Arguments or fights that you may have with your spouse or partner may be related to long-held, conditioned patterns: my conditioned mind pattern against hers. And, when you stop the conditioned mind pattern games, the entire dynamic of the relationship changes. For instance, let's say that you and you spouse argue about paying the bills—your wife forgets to write the checks. Your mind creates all sorts of negative thoughts surrounding this situation, and you begin thinking that she is incompetent and irresponsible. She fights back with thoughts about how you don't respect her, you never help, and how she probably shouldn't have married you. Your arguments are based on negative mind patterns because you give in to them.

Now, imagine that you change those patterns and quiet your mind. At bill-paying time, you are doing your exercises. On the other hand, if she hasn't read this book, her patterns remain the same. She sees what you're doing as a new tactic and her mind turns even more negative: "Why is he ignoring me? Why isn't he fighting back? It really pisses me off that he isn't getting angry. I hate this new him."

Whether with your husband or wife, friends, or associates at work, you will find that being a less irritable, calmer, less argumentative, less competitive, and less judgmental person may anger and confuse them; they may have a difficult time relating to you as a happy, nonreactive person!

Catching Yourself

When learning to watch your thoughts, you will have long periods when you are distracted and forget to pay attention to your mind. Most likely, each time you practice going back to your thoughts, you will notice that you are not doing your mantras and your mind is filled with negativity and distractions. I call this catching yourself. Don't let this discourage you. Just keep catching yourself over and over until your practice becomes second nature.

Be Persistent

The key to making this process work is persistence. Your mind will challenge you, trying to tell you that it isn't working. When that happens, go back to your mantras and your process of positive or no thoughts.

Persistence is your defense when you are tired. When I am tired, it is easy for my mind to race and I have trouble finding the energy to do my mantras, watch my thoughts, and quiet my mind—and my mind knows this all too well. There are two paths to take during these crucial times. You can give in to your mind and admit that you are too tired to do your work, or you can concentrate and, no matter how tired you are, make sure that you are doing your exercises. Your key is to be persistent and concentrate.

Also, when you are physically ill, your mind can wander to negative thoughts and you may not feel up to following your mantras. This is a time when you can get the most negative about your life circumstances and begin to think about how bad you feel and how it is impossible to be happy when you are sick. Once again, be calm and persistent. During these critical moments, use your mind for happiness without giving in to negativity, the effects of illness, or other distractions.

Hard Times

You will be tested during hard times. Nothing brings about thoughts of negativity like overdue bills, a bad week at work, troubles with your spouse, bad decisions by your kids, or sick family members. As each of these life experiences will take your thought pattern back to its original state, you will need to be persistent. No matter the circumstances, you will be better equipped to handle them with a calm mind and positive thoughts.

Be Committed

What does it take to be persistent? It takes true commitment, and true commitment is not achieved overnight. You have to believe. The only way to stay committed is to believe wholeheartedly that this can work. Think about all of the forces working against you, including the conditioning of your mind patterns over a period of years and years. Each of your family members and friends has likely grown up with the same negative mind patterns, too. The grind of daily life makes it difficult to stay committed to a new and nontraditional way of thinking.

One key to commitment is reveling in the small wins. When you slow down your thoughts for a short period of time and actually feel better, give yourself credit, and realize that it's working. Even if your practice works for five minutes or a half a day, it works. Focus on positive results to reinforce for yourself that you are on the right track.

Recognize Challenging Situations

Just like TV, texting, and phones cause distractions, certain circumstances and life situations will cause your mind to create negative and unproductive thoughts. These situational triggers cause your mind to become more active, and therefore, less calm. Triggers are different for everyone, from picking up kids from a former spouse or spending time with in-laws.

When you are able to identify situational triggers, you can be more diligent about using your mantras and quieting your mind. Instead of allowing your mind to revert back to a negative state, you know what is going to happen before it takes place and you can tell yourself that you are going to take more frequent looks at your thoughts and focus more intently on your mantra.

Here are two tricks that you can use to avoid getting caught up in the moment. First, temporarily change your mantra to fit the situation. This is called a situational mantra, as described in more detail earlier in the book. If a visit to your in-laws has been stressful in the past, you might change your mantra to: "Today is a great day. I am open to all points of view. I am not resisting anything today."

By changing your thoughts with this mantra, you change your outlook on the visit. Every time your mind says, "I can't stand his dad because he thinks he knows everything," you change it to the new mantra and you are able to accept your in-laws in a new and positive way.

Second, to fend off the effects of situational triggers, establish specific time intervals when you are going to watch your mind and make sure you are saying your mantras or quieting your mind. Decide prior to a stressful situation that you will say your mantra every five minutes and follow the plan no matter what is going on. Without even thinking about it, you will be saying your mantra constantly and your experience of a previously nerve-racking event will be positive.

Don't Do It Now

Your mind tells you that your new practice is a good idea, but not right for you. Too much is going on in your life right now to get started. You have kids to raise, a busy job, family obligations, you're putting an addition on the house, or you have a family reunion to plan. You're thinking, "I'll do it, but when I have a little more time to focus."

Yes, this process takes some work, but the great part is that it doesn't take any time. You can do it no matter what is going on in your life. When your mind says, "Don't do it now," just get started!

7

THE STORM OF EVERYDAY LIFE

How does this new way of thinking (or not thinking!) impact the issues that affect our lives every day? We do not live in a vacuum. We all face situations that challenge us, whether it is a life-changing event like the illness of a parent, or a nagging irritation such as your children fighting with each other.

This chapter discusses common challenges and how you can approach them calmly and peacefully.

Illness of a Loved One

My father has battled a terminal illness for many years, and yet, as sick as he is, I can be calm in the moment and spend time with him as a calming influence. Or, I could be a neurotic nutcase, thinking, "This is awful, woe is me, woe is him."

Regardless of my mindset, my father's situation is the

same, so being as calm as I can be during this time is helpful to both of us; the opposite can be detrimental.

The Kids Won't Stop Fighting!

Based on the feedback I've gotten on this topic, I could probably write a whole book on this alone. Children bickering and fighting will challenge even the calmest mind! The escalation point for us as parents is when we allow these events to define our experience of these moments, and therefore to define our lives.

When your kids are screaming, your natural mind reaction may be: "My life is terrible, these kids are so misbehaved. I can't get this straight. I hate this."

Instead of separating your kids' screaming from the current moment, you may allow their behavior to define the moment, and your life, when you think, "My environment is bad, I don't like what I'm doing."

To avoid focusing on the screaming, I try to bring myself back with mantras or with calming my mind. I realize that screaming and fighting is momentary, and keeping that in mind, I can diffuse these situations most effectively. I don't allow them to escalate into, "My life stinks because the kids are misbehaving."

The Daily Rush

Many people have described to me the anxiety and stress caused by the logistics of everyday family life. Our successful executive and mother of two athletic kids, Jennifer, describes this scenario perfectly: "On the home front, the thing that frustrates me the most and just drives me crazy is when I immediately plot things out in my head. For example, when we've got a game at noon, I ask myself, 'Is it home or away? We need to be there by 11:15. How long do we have to drive? We've got to be ready to walk out the door at 10:00.'

"On the other hand, my husband's reaction is simply: We've got a game at noon.

"If we need to leave at 10:00, that means we need to eat an hour earlier, and I automatically create this schedule in my head, to try and hit all those milestones that no one but me is following. We look at the clock and it's, 'Oh my God, we're behind.' Then it's manic screaming at one another to try and figure out what needs to get done fast to get everyone out the door. I'm yelling, 'Do you know what time it is? Come on! I told you half an hour ago to get your shoes on!'

"All of this may seem trivial, but it just ends up frustrating me. It's the 'get out the door on time' thing just throws me over the edge. No one but me knows what needs to be done in advance to actually get out the door, and that just drives me crazy."

The problem for Jennifer is not the screaming, the fighting, and everything that has to be done to get out the door; the problem is that she gets attached to her perceived deadline. When everything in her mind is focused on the deadline, she is anxious, and every negative thought is amplified.

The solution for Jennifer, and for every parent, is to maintain goals, while letting go of the deadlines. If your goal is to get out of the house by 8:00 a.m., that time will come and go regardless of what you do—either your kids will be on the bus or they won't. Each outcome brings another set of circumstances that you will deal with when the time comes. If they make the bus, then you come inside and clean up. If they don't make the bus, you get dressed and drive them and deal with what you have to do to get them signed in at school. The issue here is not the deadline, but the anxiety created in your mind regarding the perceived repercussions of not meeting the deadline. Very rarely is the true repercussion as bad as what you create in your mind.

You can't control how your child will react when you scream at him to tie his shoes. You can't control it when the milk spills and has to be cleaned up and your deadline is looming, and you can't control it when the baby needs a diaper change. Your mind wants to keep you thinking about all the negative outcomes if you don't hit those deadlines.

When you detach from the deadline, while maintaining your goal of getting out of the house, and you continue to participate in every event that occurs before and after 8:00 a.m., the funny thing is that you will soon make more deadlines than ever and you will do it without experiencing anxiety.

This practice can pertain to anything that involves goals and deadlines. It's great to have goals, as long as you detach from the outcomes. In other words, if you want to have $1 million in your 401(k) by the time you are fifty years old, you can take all the steps necessary to make it happen. However, either you will or you won't reach your goal, and creating anxiety around that goal for thirty years will not change the outcome.

Thoughts of success or failure around the achievement of your goals create problems. If you don't make the 8:00

a.m. deadline, then you think you are a failure and it affects your whole day, when in reality, the only thing that happened is that you didn't make it at 8:00.

The opposite is also true. If you hit your 8:00 a.m. deadline, you may get an artificial sense of self-importance and success. When in fact, all you did was make a deadline which neither improved nor worsened your lot in life. Of course, if you are like most people, that sense of accomplishment isn't nearly as strong or long-lasting as the feeling of failure if you don't.

Your Finances

Financial stresses affect us all. How can you slow the anxiety caused by uncertain situations associated with money?

Having or not having money has nothing to do with your anxiety. Anxiety is simply negative thoughts about a certain situation. Whether you have $1 in the bank or $10 million, it does not change your state of mind.

You need to disassociate your present situation related to money from negative thoughts—your money situation is what it is; anxiety doesn't make it better. Therefore, you can be poor and have positive thoughts or you can be poor and have negative thoughts.

When you start to worry about money, try a mantra such as: "I am prosperous. I am successful. I deserve to be safe and secure." When you approach your financial situation with a calm, clear mind, instead of negativity, you will be able to see solutions and ideas that were previously buried beneath your stress and anxiety.

I Don't Even Want to Get Out of Bed!

How can you change your thought process so that you have more energy and approach each day with a positive outlook? First, let's recognize that mornings can be tough, and as you will recall, a tough time to calm your mind is when you are tired. When you get up in the morning, especially without enough sleep, your mind can race in an effort to avoid engaging the day.

Gaining more energy with which to face the day is easier than you think. Before you get out of bed, take a few moments to calm your mind. Use one of the "no thoughts" exercises like the bubble or the cloud. Once you have quieted your mind, try a positive mantra before you get up, such as: "Today is a great day. I love life."

If you follow this regimen first thing in the morning, you will be surprised how much your energy level increases and your ability to cope with what the day brings improves dramatically.

My Loved One Is Annoying!

As adults, many of us are involved, or have been involved, in long-term relationships. As years go by, some of the things you once found endearing about your partner can really irritate you. For example, you may find yourself caught in thought patterns such as: "He never puts his dirty clothes in the hamper. He is always late for dinner. He used to take care of himself and now he just doesn't care. I can't remember the last time we went out. All he does is watch sports."

These issues are common, because one of the things your mind likes to do is create wanting, and your mind also loves to tell you that there is something better waiting out there for you. Negative thoughts about your spouse and your marriage are just thoughts, and your actual situation may have little to do with those thoughts. Allowing a negative dialogue to run wild through your head does absolutely nothing to enhance the quality of your relationship.

When you watch and listen to your thoughts and see negativity aimed at your partner, slow down, stop what you are doing and thinking, and breathe slowly and deeply. Try to replace that negativity with positive thoughts or with a mantra such as: "Today is a great day. I love my life. My family is my life. I love my husband. I do not judge others."

Every relationship has issues, and you can approach them with a clear mind, free of a script of pessimism running through your head. In a state of clarity and calmness, you can either let annoying behaviors go or discuss them calmly with your partner.

I Hate My Job

Many people have a hard time getting motivated to get up and go to work. They feel that every day at work is the same, and they see no light at the end of the tunnel. They may have thought patterns such as: "I get up and go to the same job every day. I get no respect at work. I definitely don't get paid enough. My boss doesn't like me and I don't like her. I am just going through the motions so I can go home. I can't believe I have to do this for fifteen more years. I don't know if I can make it."

Hating your job is similar to "hating" your marriage. Your mind fights anything that is permanent in your life, from your job, your spouse, and your kids to your personal appearance. The wanting going on in your mind includes wanting a different job, but why do you want a different job? What you really crave is happiness and acceptance of where you are right now. Truly, the grass is not greener.

Your workplace is where you spend a majority of your time, and a positive approach to work makes all the difference of all that time. Stop your negativity with a mantra such as: "I am prosperous. I love my job. Today is a great day."

8

ANSWERS TO YOUR QUESTIONS

I Am an Anxious Health Nut

I can't quiet my mind when it comes to health concerns. When I find a rash, mark, bump, or sore on me or on my child, I can't stop thinking about it. I run scenarios through my head: "Am I sick? I must have caught something. I always knew that I would get sick. My parents were always sick. I must have gotten this from them. I knew my family's health was too good to be true."

What shall I do when I am anxious about health issues?

Answer: Remember that these are only thoughts, and ask yourself which thoughts are actually factual. If you look closely, it's likely that none of them are facts. To calm your anxiety, create a mantra around positive health—"I am healthy, my family is healthy, I deserve good health"—and repeat it until you feel calm. You can then try to move to "no thoughts" by using the techniques in the book.

Saying your mantras only a few times will not be enough. If you really struggle with health concerns, negative thoughts will continue to creep in. Be diligent over the next few weeks to reinforce your positive thoughts about health.

How Long Will It Take Until I Feel Calmer and Happier?

I have started the processes, but I don't feel any different.

*How long should I expect it to take—
a week, a month, a year?*

Answer: Everyone is different. How long it will take for you to experience change depends on two things: how committed you are and what you are trying to achieve. Typically, people have a big revelation when they start the process; watching their thoughts, they learn a lot. Many of the observations made in the book will ring true after you begin watching your thoughts. At first, you experience some change simply by having the ideas in the book validated internally, then you begin the exercises and feel change begin to occur.

Your level of commitment will dictate your level of success. If you follow the suggestions and are vigilant, and you believe that they will work, you will have some immediate effects that lead to long-lasting results. When you waiver on any of the components, your results will suffer. If the process doesn't seem to be working, go back and analyze how often you are doing the work and whether you are doing it correctly. Gauge where you may be breaking down and try to increase the intensity in that particular area. It will work! The key is that you have to believe it will work. Believing in the process will dramatically speed up your results.

Obsessive Compulsive About Germs

I have a terrible anxiety about germs. I can hardly get through the day because I am deathly afraid of germs and public places. I realize that it is irrational, but I can't help it, and I am scared to take anti-anxiety medication as prescribed by my doctor. My typical thoughts are: "Public bathrooms are filthy. If I touch the door with my elbow and the sinks with a paper towel, I won't get germs. Thank goodness they have the motion-sensor faucets; but, they have manual towel dispensers. I wonder how many people have touched this sink."

How do I break my obsession with germs?

Answer: If germs were really that dangerous, we wouldn't be able to go anywhere. You will come to understand that your fear is irrational, and irrationality is thought based. No facts are involved in irrational thinking. You believe that your fear is real because it feels so real, and yet, fear is just more thoughts. To move your thoughts away from your fears, try the mantra: "I am healthy, my family is healthy. I am not afraid. I deserve good health."

I am Stuck

I have been trying to do the exercises and I thought I was having some success, but now I am stuck. It isn't working. I can't go any further with this stuff. I find myself agitated and I can't get out of it. My mind is racing. I am tired of the time commitment and I don't feel well.

What should I do?

Answer: Getting stuck and having setbacks is normal; in fact, it is expected. When you try to transform your mind, it will get more vigilant in trying to distract you and keep you in the same destructive thought patterns. Commitment is the key to your success. Remember, "I can't do this" and "this doesn't work for me" are not facts, they are only thoughts. When you feel stuck, consciously seek out more time for mantras and "no thought" exercises. If trying to do your exercises during your busy day isn't working for you, you will need to commit some time each day to get a routine going for your mind work. Also, focus your mantras around success in calming your mind: "I can calm my mind, I am at peace. I am committed to changing my thought pattern, even if it is difficult."

I am So Angry

I am always angry. I know that my life isn't that bad, and yet I can't stop feeling angry. Everything agitates me. I am constantly thinking, "I hate my life. My kids misbehave all the time. My husband is a jerk. Why did I marry him? He is so rude and obnoxious. My coffee is too cold, my shoes don't fit, my car is ugly and old, I can't stand Judy, and I need a day off. Why is that guy driving so slowly? Doesn't he know I have to be somewhere? He needs to get off the road."

How can I break the habit of anger?

Answer: A very common feeling, anger is another source of wanting. Anger makes you unable to accept what is going on right now, and it goes away when you accept the present moment instead of trying to be somewhere else. Here is a great phrase to use: "I am open to life. I accept what life has to offer. I accept what is." Once you can "accept what is" the anger will dissipate because you no longer are fighting your current circumstances that are causing the angst.

I Have the Worst Headache

My head is killing me most of the time. I often get migraines, and even when I sit in the dark, drink caffeine, and take Tylenol, nothing helps. I'm thinking, "My vision is getting blurry. There is no way I can function today."

How can I get rid of my headaches?

Answer: Usually caused by your mind and similar to anger, headaches are "wantings" intended to distract you from the present moment. You are fighting what is going on in the moment, whether it's the kids screaming, money problems, or issues with your boss. When you accept the current moment by calming your thoughts and changing them to accept what is going on, you will be amazed at how much better you will feel; the pain will go away, if you trust the process. Your mantra can be: "I release all resistance to life. I am open to life. I accept what life has to offer. I accept what is."

I Don't Want to Be Weird

I struggle with the suggestions in the book because I feel that I can't do all of this and still be normal. How can I get to a state of no thoughts, calmness, and happiness and still be a normal guy who wants to play basketball, play poker with my buddies, and sleep late? How can I hang out with friends who are gossiping over glasses of wine and still feel like one of the gang? I want to be calm and reduce my anxiety while still fitting in with my friends.

How can I make progress and still be a normal person?

Answer: Most people just want to feel better and less anxious, and to feel happier during stressful times. They want to enjoy life. By quieting your mind, you can achieve these goals by doing as much or as little as you wish with the practices outlined in this book. Of course, you could take it all the way to becoming a monk, but that is not a reasonable goal!

You will get better once you better understand and can analyze your mind. When you find that your mind is judgmental or negative, you can quietly try to change that pattern, and no one needs to know that you are doing it. Achieving a new and different state of mind can be very personal and private—you don't have to change externally to be calmer internally. If, over time, you are interested in taking it further (limiting TV, drinking less, doing yoga and meditation), then you have that choice, but it does not have to be part of the plan. You can undergo substantial internal change with no outward change, and you can even hide this book so no one will know what you are working on!

I am Depressed

I am not sure I can face the day. I feel so tired and sad. Nothing is fun and I feel dark. It is very hard for me to get out of bed. I struggle to get dressed, and I haven't been eating. Nothing interests me anymore, and I don't want to be around people. Life feels hopeless. I don't see any hope for me and my life.

How can I get over my constant fatigue and depression?

Answer: If you are depressed, it is hard to understand that depression is simply an overabundance of negative thoughts that seem so powerful and so real. And, when you see ten TV commercials for depression medications, it is no wonder that the habit of depressive thoughts is hard to break.

The easiest thing to do is to give in to our thoughts, especially when they are so strong and always present, and yet, you can learn not to surrender to them. When you feel depressed, start slowly to change your thought pattern. Making it even more difficult is a tendency to think that your thoughts are more "real" than everyone else's; that your depression is worse. The reality is that anyone can slowly, one by one, change your thought pattern. Each time you have a negative thought, repeat something like: "I can be happy in this moment. I feel relaxed and happy. I love life and embrace life. I am ready for all that life has to offer."

I Can't Listen to My iPod?

I want to listen to music and podcasts while I am remodeling my kitchen and doing other work that I don't want to do.

Why can't I listen to my iPod while I am doing chores at home?

Answer: The problem is not the iPod, it is your approach to kitchen remodeling and other household chores that is the problem. Your mind is telling you: "This job sucks. I can't believe I have to do this. Why won't my wife let me hire someone? Doesn't she care that I work all week and the last thing I want to do is do work on the kitchen?"

Because your mind tells you that you hate the job, you want to put on the iPod, but that is only a distraction from your negative thoughts and it allows those thoughts to continue automatically and subconsciously. While you may believe that iPod will make the experience endurable, it is actually helping to maintain a negative thought pattern and embed it deep into your mind's subconscious, making that particular pattern of thinking even harder to break.

Try positive mantras for the first half hour of your work on the kitchen, and if you feel good about the job and are in a positive state, then listen to the iPod, focusing on the music and thoroughly enjoying it. Remember, while listening to your music or the radio or TV, you still need to periodically check your thoughts, and if they change back to negative, turn off the music and return to your mantras.

I Worry All the Time

If I don't worry, my kids will run into the street. How can I ensure that I am doing everything I need to do if I don't worry? You tell us that worrying is bad, but isn't there some type of worry that keeps us out of trouble or from getting hurt?

How can I just not worry at all?

Answer: Worry of any kind is unproductive. Nothing positive comes from worry. We often need to make informed decisions, but that is not worry. For example, if we see scary people in a dark alley, rather than worrying about it, we decide not to walk down that alley instead of running all sorts of scenarios through our heads: "Are they going to mug me? What happens if they jump out in front of me? Am I fast enough to get away?"

A head full of worry and anxiety does not help a clear, decisive mind to make sound decisions that help one avoid bad situations. If you see a strange lump on your leg, use good judgment and get it checked out, instead of giving in to thoughts such as "Do I have cancer? Am I going to die? Am I going to be here to see my children grow up?" None of this is helpful and none of the "worry" questions are facts.

My Life Is Worse Than Most People's

My life has been terrible lately. I can't seem to catch a break. I lost my job, my husband left me, I have difficult relationships with my kids, and my parents are very sick. I understand your concepts for normal people with normal lives, but that is not me.

How can I possibly be happy with so much that is negative in my life?

Answer: "My life has been terrible lately" is only a thought or a perspective. In reality, your life is simply a series of experiences, and your labels of good or bad are judgments made by your mind. You interpret and judge the events of your life as good, bad, endurable, or unacceptable according to your thought patterns. Remember, situations are not good or bad, it is how we perceive them that define them in our mind. The same incident may be perceived as "good" by one person and "bad" by another. Try to refrain from judging or labeling any particular event or circumstance.

Like depression, the focus on what is terrible about your life can be tough to get beyond when you are in the middle of it. The key is to be diligent about mantras and have a conviction that it can work. Your mind will challenge you and tell you that the bills, the fights with your spouse, the job, and the family problems are real and won't go away by just changing your thoughts. However, you are in control of how you view each of those situations. A great mantra could be "I can make this work. I believe in my right to happiness. I love my life and look forward to each day. I am thankful for what I have. Everything around me is filled with goodness."

Does This New Way of Thinking Conflict with My Religion?

I grew up in a very Christian household. We went to church every weekend. I went to eight years of Sunday school. I was taught to turn to God for everything, I pray when I need help and I have a lot of guilt around trying to change my way of thinking. So, even if I think this could help me, I feel like it may go against everything I was taught since I was a kid.

How do I harmonize my religious beliefs with my new way of life?

Answer: None of the processes and practices in this book conflict with any religion, although some of the mind concepts have some similarities to elements of Buddhism. The purpose of the book is to help people calm their minds, reduce anxiety, and lead a happier life—and those concepts are consistent with any religion. If there is any inconsistency, it may revolve around who is in control of your happiness, as some religions may rely on faith or God to create a path to happiness. Clearly, this book places all of the control for your own happiness squarely in your hands.

About the Author

Michael Traina is an entrepreneur, a father, a husband and a coach. Most of all, he is just a normal guy. Born in Chicago, he was adopted by a loving Midwestern family and grew up with three siblings, living in various places including Indiana, Pennsylvania and Massachusetts. He said, "My upbringing was about as normal as it could be, with days filled with sports, school, playing outside, and watching TV.

"My father began his career as a history professor and ended it as a university administrator. Consequently , our dinner table conversations involved healthy debate where freedom of expression and divergent ideas were encouraged. We were never forced to believe what our parents believed; instead, they encouraged us to think for ourselves and come to our own conclusions."

Traina credits this free thinking environment with his ability to embrace change throughout his life and career. "I learned that just because your parents, mentors, or teachers believe a certain way should not determine what you think. I also know that change is possible. We are not the same person at forty that we were in our twenties, and we should constantly reexamine our beliefs, the origin of those beliefs and the logic in them. By doing so, we can make critical changes to ensure that we are living the most full and open life that we can.

This book is a result of decades of critical thinking on the author's part and a lot of trial and error. It was not until he truly embraced that there are many paths to a happy life that he was able to look objectively at his own life and make changes. He also tries to impart these concepts to his five children in the hope that they will find happiness sooner in life than he did and without as many missteps.

Michael Traina would love to hear from you! Email him at whatifs@fivekidspublishing.com

CPSIA information can be obtained at www.ICGtesting.com
Printed in the USA
BVOW04s1144020215

386003BV00005B/7/P